WALKING TOGETHER WITH GOD THROUGH DEATH AND GRIEF

EXPERIENCING GOD'S
COMFORTING LOVE

WALKING TOGETHER WITH GOD THROUGH DEATH AND GRIEF

Joycelyn V. Gilbert

Xulon Press

Xulon Press
2301 Lucien Way #415
Maitland, FL 32751
407.339.4217
www.xulonpress.com

© 2022 by Joycelyn V. Gilbert

All rights reserved solely by the author. The author guarantees all contents are original and do not infringe upon the legal rights of any other person or work. No part of this book may be reproduced in any form without the permission of the author.

Due to the changing nature of the Internet, if there are any web addresses, links, or URLs included in this manuscript, these may have been altered and may no longer be accessible. The views and opinions shared in this book belong solely to the author and do not necessarily reflect those of the publisher. The publisher therefore disclaims responsibility for the views or opinions expressed within the work.

Unless otherwise indicated, Scripture quotations taken from the King James Version (KJV) – public domain.

Scripture quotations taken from the Holy Bible, New International Version (NIV). Copyright © 1973, 1978, 1984, 2011 by Biblica, Inc.™. Used by permission. All rights reserved.

Scripture quotations taken from the English Standard Version (ESV). Copyright © 2001 by Crossway, a publishing ministry of Good News Publishers. Used by permission. All rights reserved.

Scripture quotations taken from the New American Standard Bible (NASB). Copyright © 1960, 1962, 1963, 1968, 1971, 1972, 1973, 1975, 1977, 1995 by The Lockman Foundation. Used by permission. All rights reserved.

Paperback ISBN-13: 978-1-66286-766-8
Hardcover ISBN-13: 978-1-66287-405-5
Ebook ISBN-13: 978-1-66286-767-5

Preface

THIS JOURNAL IS my own personal grief journey from my very own experiences I am living every day. It is a journey I want to share to help others navigate everyday life, after the death of a loved one–as my family and I experienced death in what I would call the most surprising and painful way. I want to also confirm that without trusting God and allowing Him to be the center of my grief, this journey would have been much more difficult.

The process may not be the same for everyone, but this is the mirror of my life that I see every day. I am writing this journal to honor my beloved husband Dwight A. Gilbert as he was loving, caring, kind, gracious, and thoughtful by always putting others before himself.

Finally, I am writing this journal to understand, accept, and properly grieve Dwight's untimely death, to support our daughter Sarai in her grief and at the same time to help other families and individuals who are grieving the loss of a loved one. You can journal, as well.

I trust that this journal will provide support and guidance as you journey towards closure. Closure does not mean the journey ends; it means the process might be easier to bear. -Joycelyn

Table Of Contents

Introduction xi
Stage 1 of Grief 1
Week One
    Day 1 2
    Day 2 5
    Day 3 9
    Day 4 11
    Day 5 14
    Day 6 18
Stage 2 of Grief 20
Week Two
    Day 1 21
    Day 2 23
    Day 3 27
    Day 4 29
    Day 5 31
    Day 6 33
Stage 3 of Grief 34
Week Three
    Day 1 35
    Day 2 37
    Day 3 39
    Day 4 41
    Day 5 43
    Day 6 45
Stage 4 of Grief 46

Week Four
- Day 1 47
- Day 2 49
- Day 3 52
- Day 4 54
- Day 5 56
- Day 6 59

Stage 5 of Grief 60

Week Five:
- Day 1 61
- Day 2 64
- Day 3 66
- Day 4 68
- Day 5 70
- Day 6 73

Final Word 74

Endnotes 79

INTRODUCTION
Broken, Numb, Weak, and in Shock

IN THE BEGINNING God created the heavens and the earth.... Then God said, "Let us make mankind in our image, in our likeness, so that they may rule over the fish in the sea and the birds in the sky, over the livestock and all the wild animals, and over all the creatures that move along the ground." So God created mankind in his own image, in the image of God he created them; male and female he created them. (Genesis 1:1, 26-27 NASB)

Dwight can be described as a man who appeared to be a picture of good health. He was complimented about his love for God, his physique, smile, and his healthy eating habits. Dwight was not sick as far as we knew. He had a socially balanced life, interacted with others with humility, mentally stable, always smiling, and he never complained about any known illness prior to when I received the call that something went wrong. We had just had a beautiful time that morning. I do recall that Dwight's eyes were lighter than usual, and his skin appeared really radiant.

I mentioned it to him, and he answered, "Oh, it must be the soap. I told him he looked and smelled good."

As we drove, I told him I would wait downstairs for him, as I waited within thirty minutes I received a telephone call that something was wrong with Dwight. I immediately rushed to his rescue. As I approached where he lay, I was prevented from seeing him. Within an hour after arriving at the Emergency Room, Dwight was pronounced deceased. The attending doctor presented his wedding band to me; a ring he enjoyed wearing and never left home without it. I experienced the chilling hands of death while waiting patiently for Dwight to return to the car after his appointment.

When Dwight died suddenly, I was so broken. I was numb, weak, and in complete utter shock. Prior to his death, reading the Bible, praying, and fasting were a part of my daily routine. When I read anything biblical that intrigued me, I immediately shared it with Dwight. Dwight was my partner. I bounced scripture verses off him and he gladly discussed them with me. We knew God had put us together to strengthen and encourage one another.

When Dwight passed, I was in shock. I couldn't read my Bible, pray, or fast. I just wanted to lay down and hope this dream would be over. For several months, I abandoned everything about God. Yes, my faith was shaken. How could this happen? We were so faithful.

I laid in bed unable to move for several months of intense grief. Finally, I reached for what I knew—the Bible. I had missed so many books, chapters, and verses to complete my goal of reading the Bible in one year. I was in physical pain from my heartache as I stretched myself to reach for my Bible. It was the most difficult stretch I had ever done.

As I held the Bible, I said, "I believe everything in this book, and I will hold onto it."

The Bible felt weighty in my hands. As difficult and painful as it was, I slowly opened the Bible. Miraculously, the page it opened to was Psalm 118. As I read this psalm, the Holy Spirit spoke to my spirit, my inner man, as clear as a sunny day, "[You] shall not die, but live, and declare the works of the Lord" (Psalm 118:17).

Though I still did not understand why this had happened, I knew God was not done with me yet.

Losing a close family member or friend brings intense grief that can leave us physically, emotionally, and spiritually numb, weak, and in shock. Yes, our faith can be shaken as we instinctively ask God why.

Describe your initial reactions to the death of a close family member or friend.

REFLECTIVE QUESTIONS:

How did it affect you physically?

_____

_____

How did it affect you mentally?

How did it affect you emotionally?

How did it affect you spiritually?

How was your relationship with others?

How was your relationship with God?

Introduction

Pray:

Father God, I know You have control of everything. You created heaven and the earth, You made man in Your own image, and You have great power. I do not understand why this has happened. I feel so broken. I stretch my hands out to You. I know You will comfort me and give me understanding of Your plan. Lord, please be patient with me so I can live and not die and move on to declare Your works as You have designed me to do. Amen

Stage 1 of Grief

Denial

THIS IS THE first of our reactions to any form of sudden loss. It is very common to try and initially deny the event in order to subconsciously avoid sadness, or the thought of pending mental struggles. People in denial often withdraw from their normal social behavior and become isolated. It is a coping mechanism that helps us survive the loss.[1]

In this stage, the world becomes meaningless and overwhelming. Life makes no sense. We are in a state of shock and denial. We go numb. We wonder how we can go on, if we can go on, why we should go on. We try to find a way to simply get through each day. Denial helps us to pace our feelings of grief. There is a grace in denial. As you accept the reality of the loss and start to ask yourself questions, you are unknowingly beginning the healing process. You are becoming stronger, and the denial is beginning to fade. However, as you proceed, all the feelings you were denying begin to surface.[2]

WEEK ONE
DAY 1
One Day at a Time

> Where no counsel is, the people fall: but in the multitude of counselors there is safety. (Proverbs 11:14 KJV)

THIS SCRIPTURE IS important because it speaks of the safety we receive in the midst of counsel. Counsel could mean getting support from family, friends, church members, group support, and therapy. Honestly, you feel safe when you are in the company of others, but sometimes during your bereavement, these supporters believe you cannot do anything for yourself. Naturally, you should not make any hasty financial decisions or plans with specific deadlines during this time. Her intentions were good, but my sister Carol went ahead and arranged a therapy session for me without consulting me. I went along with her plans, she wanted me to be myself again.

After attending the sessions for four weeks, the physician advised me to save my money as he told me I did not need to come back anymore. This was so far from the truth. I did need support, but obviously, it was not to come from this direction. I guess he did not recognize the depression, the pain, the sleepless nights, and the agony I was in at the time. I was suffering from grief, depression, and felt as if I was going to a place from where I could not return.

Luckily, I was contacted by a friend that was starting a support group. This was so ironic as she herself had not experienced the death of a spouse. This group started with seven bereaved women, some very young and some not so young. These sessions got me out of bed and the level of support from the other women was overwhelming. As I heard their stories, I realized my situation was painful, yet I was in a better place. I attended sessions twice a month. These sessions became like a cast that holds broken bones together until they heal.

However, as the meeting times fizzled out, I realized I had to find other things to occupy my space and time to save myself. I needed to figure out what was needed to get my life back on track.

We are very vulnerable during the beginning stages of grief. Friends and family don't know what to say so they try to do things for us.

REFLECTIVE QUESTIONS:

If you are in the initial stages of grief, how have others tried to "help you"?

_____

_____

You may be tempted to let them, but be careful you are not pushed into something that is not what you want or truly need. Has this happened to you? _____
How did you respond?

_____

_____

It might be helpful to connect with a grief support group focused on the same loss you have experienced (spouse, child, parent). Being with a Christian support group other than family and friends gives you the freedom to be open and honest about your feelings.

Pray:

Father, please remind me daily that You love me. Strengthen me when I am weak. As I listen to and sing Christian songs, I feel Your presence and my weariness disappears. It is in these times I know I am not alone. I humbly ask You to continue to speak with clear directions on how I am to move forward. I know You used imperfect people such as Leah, Rahab, Naomi, Martha, and Sarah, so I know You can use me, too. I know You have made a way of escape from the depression that is trying to overcome me. I pray You would direct me to the grief supporters You are sending my way. In the name of Jesus Christ, I pray. Amen.

Day 2
The Spirit of Worry

> Take therefore no thought for the morrow, for tomorrow shall take thought for the things of itself. Sufficient unto the day is evil thereof. (Matthew 6:34 KJV)

At first, I had help with the immediate decisions that had to be made like the funeral arrangements. I am so grateful to Lesa who took the lead. I was advised not to make any rash or quick major decisions. However, once everyone went home and I knew I was going to need to begin to function pretty much on my own, I began to worry about my life from here on.

How should I take my first step? How can I move forward? What about our daughter, the bills, and everything else that began demanding my attention?

Dwight, my wisdom decision-maker, was not here to help me. At this point, I could not decide how to move forward with my life. I moved from my mom's house to my brother Anthony, Pamela Mirage and Antinique house. However, worry followed me and the decisions still had to be made.

Then, I recalled what Jesus said in Matthew 6:25-34. I pulled out my Bible and read again what He told to His followers about the cure for worry.

"For this reason I say to you, do not be worried [or stop being worried] about your life, as to what you will eat or what you will drink; nor for your body, as to what you will put on. Is life not more than food, and the body more than clothing? Look at the birds of the sky, that they do not sow, nor reap, nor gather crops into barns, and yet your heavenly Father feeds them. Are you not much more important than they? And which of you by worrying can add a single day to his life's span? And why are you worried about clothing? Notice how the lilies of the field grow; they do not labor nor do they spin thread for cloth, yet I say to you that not even Solomon in all his glory clothed himself like one of these. But if God so clothes the grass of the field, which is alive today and tomorrow is thrown into the furnace, will He not much more clothe you? You of little faith! Do not worry then, saying, 'What are we to eat?' or 'What are we to drink?' or 'What are we to wear for clothing?' For the Gentiles eagerly seek all these things; for your heavenly Father knows that you need all these things. But [continually] seek first His kingdom and His righteousness, and all these things will be provided to you. So do not worry about tomorrow; for tomorrow will worry about itself. Each day has enough trouble of its own. (NASB)[3]

I noticed the questions Jesus asked His listeners and wondered how I would answer them. How would you answer Jesus if He asked you these questions?

Day 2

Reflective Questions:

Is life not more than food, and the body more than clothing?
Are you not much more important than they [birds of the air]?
And which of you by worrying can add a single day to your life's span?
What did Jesus say was the cure for worry?

_____

_____

Does this mean we should not take care of our responsibilities?

Seeking God's righteousness first means doing things His way because His way will always be the right way. I have discovered by reading the Bible, studying God's instructions, and then praying to seek His direction will bring me peace of mind. This does not mean hiding my head under the pillow or not paying my bills. It means taking one day at a time and dealing with one issue at a time as I seek His guidance and the godly counsel He sends our way.

Pray:

Father, please show me how to seek You first, take one day at a time, and one issue at a time to remove the spirit of worry off of me. Bless me with the supernatural peace only You can give me to deal with _____ death. Help me to move forward and handle the important decisions Your way. In Jesus' name, Amen.

Day 3
The First Visitation

Let all things be done decently and in order.
(1 Corinthians 14:40)

I GRIEVED SO hard; it was extremely painful. During my grief, I had completely abandoned our home, living between my parents and brother and sister-in-law's homes. I was comfortable and was allowed to grieve peacefully without interruptions. Except when they thought I should eat or go in the pool. Oh my gosh, I needed support from friends and family.

Remember, do not rely on your own strength, but cast all your cares on the Lord Jesus Christ because He cares for you.

I still missed Dwight and was in shock. Honestly, I thought I would lose my mind. As I write this passage, I know if I did not have a personal relationship with God, I do not know where I would be today.

I planned with my sister-in-law Pamela to visit Dwight's gravesite. As we arrived, I was emotionally distraught. We walked to where we thought Dwight was, but we could not find him. So many new graves but no names. This was on a Sunday.

Monday morning, still emotionally grieved and in shock, I telephoned the cemetery's office and cried as I told the nice lady I could not find my husband. She begged me to calm down and promised she would place a temporary headstone with his initial DG. When I returned to the gravesite, I was able to identify Dwight's resting place. While this was a bittersweet moment for me, it demonstrated how all things must be done decently and in order. Each person has a right to identify their loved ones regardless of the circumstance of their death. We must remember that others' lives are affected by what we do as well.

Pray:

Thank You, Lord, for granting me supernatural faith so I am able to help others know that part of the healing process is to conduct our affairs in decency and order. Lord, help us to understand we should always strive to do what is right even when we are in pain. Lord, help us to remain steadfast in our faith daily. Thank You, Lord, for always bringing relief when we feel that there is no way out. Amen.

Day 4
Humility

> Submit yourselves therefore to God.... Draw nigh to God, and he will draw nigh to you. (James 4:7-8 KJV)

I CONTINUED TO submit myself to God as this journey was just too difficult for me to handle by myself. No matter how much support I received from family, friends, and colleagues it was just not enough. There was still a void and an emptiness within me that their support could not fill.

You will definitely feel the care and support from your loved ones. Yet, a void still exists that they are not meant to fill. It is at this point, you must choose to submit yourself under the mighty hand of God.

The Psalmist says in Psalm 62:5, "My soul, wait only upon God and silently submit to Him; for my hope and expectation are from Him" (NASB).

How do we submit? By reading His Word, being in constant prayer which includes talking and listening to Him, and listening to uplifting music that is full of praise, hope, and expectation.

Submission requires humility and surrendering our ways to His ways. When we choose to submit to the Lord in all we do and surrender every part of our lives to Him, we will be rewarded.

Psalm 25:9 says, "He guides the humble in what is right and teaches them his way" (NASB). No matter how difficult our circumstances, how trying our testimony, or how fearful the future feels, we can rely on the promise that when we submit to Him and are humble before God, He will lift us up.

God's promises are true. I take great comfort in these promises because I know no matter what happens around me, He will give me grace, mercy, guidance, and wisdom.

Reflective Questions:

Is the journey you are on too difficult for you to handle by yourself?
Are you finding even the support of friends and family still leaves a void in your life?

Beware of the self-help suggestions the world and others may offer. Only God knows what you really need.
What kind of self-help has the world or others offered you?

_____

_____

Micah 6:8 says, "He has told you, mortal one, what is good; And what does the Lord require of you but to do justice, to love kindness, and to walk humbly with your God?" (NASB). Will you choose to humbly submit to the Lord in all you do and to surrender every part of your life to Him?

Reread the scriptures above and use them to help you submit yourself in humility to God.

Remember, this important warning given in Proverbs 14:12,

> "There is a way which seems right to a person, but its end is the way of death" (NASB).

> "For My thoughts are not your thoughts, nor are your ways My ways," declares the LORD. (Isaiah 55:8 NASB)

Pray:

Father God, I thank You for accepting me as Your child. I know You can use a broken vessel to be a light to someone else. Dear Lord, I submit myself under Your authority and yield to You all that I am. Please give me the guidance and wisdom I need to move forward and do what You have designed me to do. In Jesus' name I pray. Amen.

Day 5
God Is Always With Us
We Are Never Alone

> Have not I commanded thee? Be strong and of good courage; be not afraid, neither be thou dismayed: for the Lord thy God is with thee whithersoever thou goest. (Joshua 1:9 KJV)

IT WAS NOT a special occasion. I missed my Dwight and just wanted to visit his gravesite. However, as I thought about going, I felt my body aching and I became nervous. My mind said I could not do it, not today. My body said lay down, it's just too much for you, not today.

At that moment, I needed God's intervention. I cried and prayed in the spirit. Talking to God as a dear friend, I explained my desire and boldly asked for His sustaining grace if I was to go alone to the gravesite. The Holy Spirit spoke to me and said go. It was painful as I got up and got dressed. I could not even see where I was going as I drove towards the gravesite as the flow of tears washed down my face.

As I entered the cemetery, a few vehicles were just departing as I arrived. I was afraid as I walked by faith towards the gate alone. I thought everyone had left. I recalled Dwight's words to be aware of my surroundings and never walk alone.

The security guard, Mr. Moncur, approached me. I saw compassion in his eyes.

He kept his distance and asked, "Where are you going?"

With large teardrops flowing from my eyes, I said, "To visit my husband."

He said kindly, "I am off my shift, but I will walk with you and stay nearby to give you privacy."

This was God's amazing grace at work. I was able to sit and talk with Dwight about life's challenges and the events that had recently taken place. I knew Dwight had died and would not hear or answer me, but I was comforted after I yielded to the direction of the Holy Spirit.

I miss Dwight as I am sure you miss your loved one. I wrote these words to confirm we will be okay because God's Word promises we are never alone when we trust Him.

This first time I went to Dwight's gravesite was God confirming His promise through the kindly security guard.

Read this amazing verse in Zephaniah 3:17**.** "The Lord your God is in your midst, a mighty one who will save; he will rejoice over you with gladness; he will quiet you by his love; he will exult over you with loud singing."

How does this comfort your heart and ease your anxiety?

_____

_____

God continually confirmed His presence in my life through various means. I was learning to listen to His voice and respond to His prompting knowing He would never send me down the wrong path.

Read Isaiah 30:21. "Whether you turn to the right or to the left, your ears will hear a voice behind you, saying 'This is the way; walk in it.'"

Are you learning to listen for His still small voice?

God knew my heart and what and when I needed to be reminded of His presence. He reminded me of the promises Jesus made to His disciples before He ascended into heaven. In Matthew 28:20, Jesus said, "And be sure of this: I am with you always, even to the end of the age."

> "And I will ask the Father, and he will give you another Helper, to be with you forever, even the Spirit of truth, whom the world cannot receive, because it neither sees Him nor knows Him. You know Him, for He dwells with you and will be in you." (John: 14:16-17)

Day 5

Remember the promise in Psalm 145:18 and call on Him in prayer. "The Lord is near to all who call on him, to all who call on him in truth."

Pray:

Father, in the name of Jesus Christ, I thank You for Your divine and supernatural protection when it is needed most. Thank You for lifting me up and letting me stand in awe of Your continuous presence. Amen.

Day 6
My Journal

"I will never leave you nor forsake you."
- God's Promise

As you journeyed with me through this first week of reading my story, I shared with you some of God's great and precious promises that helped guide me as I dealt with the overwhelming grief of losing my beloved spouse. These memories were journaled in my heart. Now, it is your turn to journal your memories of your journey. Review these precious promises. Choose and record the ones that fit with your memories.

Psalm 118:17, Psalm 91:1, Psalm 37:23, Isaiah 41:10, Psalm 16:33, James 4:7-8, Psalm 25:9, Joshua 1:9, Zephaniah 3:17, Isaiah 30:21, Matthew 28:20, John: 14:16-17, Psalm 145:18.

_____

_____

_____

_____

Day 6

Stage 2 of Grief

Anger

People who are grieving often become upset with the person or situation which puts them in their grief state. After all, their life could now be in complete disarray. The path of least resistance is anger as opposed to facing the consequences of a loss head on. The anger is often focused toward the deceased for leaving that person behind and unable to cope. Other times people become angry at themselves if they feel they could have done something more to stop the loss from happening.[4]

> "The fact is that when you admit that you can't blame anyone or anything else, you begin to blame yourself. The human mind gives up trying to find an executioner, but still it must blame someone. Anger that is not expressed tends to turn inward and, instead, attacks the very one who feels it. You move from anger and guilt into depression."
>
> **Kate McGahan**[5]

WEEK TWO
DAY 1
When You Walk Humbly with God

He hath shewed thee, O man, what is good,
and what doth the Lord require of thee, but
to do justly, and to love mercy, and to walk
humbly with thy God? (Micah 6:8 KJV)

DWIGHT AND I walked for almost sixteen years five days of the week either in the morning or the evening. After Dwight's death, I could not bring myself to walk anymore. We always talked about walking with God under the open heaven. Dwight often said look at God's face as we marveled when we looked in the distance at what appeared to be the sky meeting the beach.

> Take a walk today and look for God's face all around you. Take the time to communicate with God as you walk with Him.

Today, months later, I decided I had to keep moving as Dwight would not want me to be stagnant and definitely this is not God's plan for me. This was a challenge for me. As I got dressed, I felt the need to see Dwight. I got in the vehicle and drove to the flower shop, purchased seven yellow roses for Dwight's headstone and this gave me comfort. Going to Dwight's gravesite in some strange way gave me the courage to walk.

As I went to our usual parking spot near the beach and walked towards Goodman's Bay, I recalled Charles Wesley's "Father, I Stretch My Hands To Thee No other Help I know; If Thou Withdraw Thyself from me, Ah! Whither shall I go." As I continued to walk at a slow pace, I felt God's presence. Definitely, I was not alone. As I walked on the sand along the shoreline, I saw God's handiwork from a different point of view. It looked like the sky and heaven were connected. I used this opportunity to communicate with God. At this point, my pace increased and at the end, I took a deep breath and said, "Thank You, Lord. You did it again."

Pray:

"Our Father Who Art in Heaven Hallowed Be Thy Name" Matthew 6:9. Thank You dear Lord for giving me the courage to step boldly with You today, for leading me along the way, and for letting me know that if I take one step, You will walk with me the rest of the way. Amen.

Day 2
Walking and Living in the Supernatural

> He that dwelleth in the secret place of the most High shall abide under the shadow of the Almighty. (Psalm 91:1 KJV)

As time went by, I realized I had to begin to appreciate I was dwelling in the secret place of the Most High God and could move from point A to point B while abiding under the shadow of the Almighty. I needed to progress so I could live and not die in both the physical and spiritual realms.

Physically, I needed groceries. My plan was to get up at the crack of dawn to shop for groceries wearing a disguise. Wearing a baseball cap and sunglasses, I waited patiently for the store to open and walked nervously from aisle to aisle hoping not to run into any familiar faces. This was my first time out shopping since Dwight's death.

As I quickly gathered the few items on my list, I felt strange and out of place. Then, I recalled I was under the shadow of the Almighty and had divine coverage and protection while I was in a supernatural hiding place. My first shopping experience went smoothly.

I had made an important first step that day to moving forward with God.

"You who sit down in the High God's presence, spend the night in Shaddai's shadow, Say this: "GOD, you're my refuge. I trust in you and I'm safe!" That's right—he rescues you from hidden traps, shields you from deadly hazards. His huge, outstretched arms protect you—under them you're perfectly safe; his arms fend off all harm."–Eugene H. Peterson

This translation of Psalm 37:23 assured me that if I would walk in step with God and choose to stay on His path for me, then I could confidently begin to move forward knowing even if I stumbled, God had a hold of my hand.

God patiently reassured me day by day of His supernatural presence in my life.

You can experience that same reassurance. Here are some of the other verses that continued to reassure me as I chose to walk with God and acknowledge His supernatural presence in my life no matter what I had to face in my life.

Read Isaiah 41:10. "Fear thou not; for I am with thee: be not dismayed; for I am thy God: I will strengthen thee; yea, I will help thee; yea, I will uphold thee with the right hand of my righteousness" (KJV).

Day 2

Reflective Questions:

What is causing you to fear moving forward with your life? How are you going to respond when this fear tries to rise up and attack you?

_____

_____

Read Psalm 16:11. "Thou wilt shew me the path of life: in thy presence is fullness of joy; at thy right hand there are pleasures for evermore" (KJV).
How has this verse encouraged you today?

_____

_____

Read Psalm 100:2. "Serve the LORD with gladness: come before his presence with singing" (KJV).
Will you lift up your hands and come before His presence with singing as you start your day?

Pray:

Father, thank You for allowing me to be sheltered under Your shadow and extending Your secret place where I can come and feel safe and secure. I will come before Your presence today and every day with singing. My desire is to continue to serve

You with my life. Please show me the path You have placed before me. Thank You, dear Lord, for holding my hand and walking with me supernaturally. Amen

DAY 3
God Is Rejoicing with Joy
When Goals Are Accomplished

The Lord thy God in the midst of thee is mighty; he will save, He will rejoice over thee with joy; He will rest in His love, He will joy over thee with singing. (Zephaniah 3:17)

THIS SCRIPTURE REMINDS me of Colossians 2:5, "God is not with us in the flesh but in the Spirit joying and beholding your order, and the steadfastness of your faith in Christ." With these scriptures in mind, on election day, I recalled every election for the last fifteen years. Dwight and I would vote very, very early, meeting the same people almost in the same voting position, year after year, especially Tanya and her mother.

However, I did not get up early, but several hours later than usual. It was extremely hot. I struggled to leave the house, but I remembered Dwight's words, "vote with your heart." I stood alone, I felt alone, and I cried alone even though I was in the midst of hundreds of people. Yet, I knew God was watching over me. Lesa had called the day before saying she had an umbrella for me. I used it to hide my face. I moved as the line advanced to the voting station alone. I wanted to leave, yet, I had to rest in God's love and vote for Dwight. As I reached the front door, I felt the pain. This is where we always separated, but today there was no separation. I was alone. I did my oath and voted. As I left the voting zone, I knew the Lord my God was rejoicing over that small faith of accomplishment, and He was singing with joy over me.

Reflective Questions:

Are you finding it difficult to do the things you used to do with your loved one?

How would your loved one want you to handle each situation?

_____

_____

Pray:

Father, thank You for the Holy Spirit, and thank You for helping me stand firm. Thank You for giving me the strength to stand when I felt like I should quit. In Jesus' name I pray, Amen.

Day 4
Having a Meek Spirit

The meek will He guide in judgment: and the meek will He teach his way. (Psalm 25:9)

This scripture has never meant much to me until I returned to my home that I had abandoned for several months and everyone else returned to their normal lives.

During this time, it was extremely difficult to be alone and the only people available to keep me company was my two-year-old grandniece Jazmyn (Jazzy- she stayed very close to me in the bed, and I felt comforted by her presence), and three nieces one seven, two eleven-year-olds, Halo, Briette, and Ameya respectively. I cannot confirm if they came reluctantly or willingly. Now, I find myself laughing silently and recall saying, "Look what I have come to God does have a sense of humor." The young children with their meek spirits caused me to have some sleep and feel secure. This is when I began to own my brokenness but did not want pity. I know they did not understand what was happening, they just knew that Uncle Dwight was not there.

I also recalled that as soon as they walked in the door the first time, they wanted the Wi-Fi password, and immediately they ventured into another bedroom. The freedom of social media I guessed, yet they served a purpose that I understood and appreciated. This is God guiding and teaching me how to accept His divine favor.

Reflective Question:

How has God been guiding you to accept His divine favor?

_____

_____

Pray:

Father, in the name of Jesus, I thank You for letting me see how You are taking care of us in the strangest ways. Thank You, Jesus, for opening our hearts to accept that favor comes in small packages and that as You promise in Your Word You will never forsake us. Help me, dear Lord, to continue to trust and believe Your promises.

Day 5
My Secret Place

He that dwelleth in the secret place of the most High shall abide under the shadow of the Almighty. (Psalm 91:1)

MY SECRET PLACE during my grief was staying in the presence of the Lord. After I was finally able to strengthen my spiritual walk with God, I felt a need to comply with Hebrew 10:25 and not forsake the assembling of ourselves together. I asked my Mommy Ismay Delores Seymour to accompany me to our family church, United Christian Cathedral, Flamingo Gardens. I just could not go alone, and I did not have the strength to attend Vision of Hope Cathedral, Church of God where Dwight and I had attended.

Imagine God and your mother together. As I walked into the sanctuary, I felt the presence of the Holy Spirit. I felt Psalm 91 equipped. I had repeated this Psalm with Creflo and Taffi Dollar Confessions for almost two years. My girlfriend, Admirah, called when Dwight died and said those confessions were preparing me for this season in my life.

At church, I felt at home, yet I was broken as this was the church where I married the love of my life, Dwight. It was an emotional service. The first congregational hymn was Lead Me, Guide Me by Doris Aker, our wedding ceremony congregational hymn.

This was confirmation of Dwight's final prayer over Sarai and me. Keep them safe Lord and bless Joyce. God take care of Joyce for me. As time has passed, Psalm 91, a scripture my mommy gave me more than thirty years ago, along with Psalm 23 that Dwight and I read on the morning that he died, are my daily confessions.

Memorize and make Psalm 91:1 your daily confession and learn to dwell in that secret place with Almighty God.

Pray:

Father, in the name of Jesus, I thank You so much for equipping me to handle events that are unexpected. Thank You, Lord, for walking with me from when I took my first step and keeping me safe now as I move forward with You, Amen.

Day 6
My Journal
Walking with God

He that dwelleth in the secret place of the most High shall abide under the shadow of the Almighty. (Psalm 91:1)

As I wrote this week's passages, I realized once again that if I did not have a personal relationship with God, I do not know where I would be today. Walking with Him has helped me to move forward so I can help others by sharing His faithfulness.

As you journeyed with me as I walked with God through the stages of my grief, think about where your journey with God has taken you. Record how knowing God's presence and faithfulness has given you what you need to continue moving forward.

_____

_____

_____

_____

STAGE 3 OF GRIEF
Bargaining

"THE THIRD STAGE of grief is Bargaining. This is when those who are grieving are reaching out to the universe to make the pain go away. It is actually very normal, and largely considered to be a sign that they are beginning to comprehend their situation. People will often try to make a deal, or promise to do anything, if the pain will be taken away."[6]

You are struggling to find meaning to what happened and trying to gain some control over your life.

> "Understand there's no right or wrong way to grieve, including anticipatory grief. It's like the ocean. It ebbs and it flows. There can be moments of calm. But out of nowhere, it can feel like you're drowning."
>
> Dana Arcuri
>
> Sacred Wandering: Growing Your Faith In The Dark[7]

WEEK THREE
DAY 1
The Unexpected Season

> To everything there is a season, and a time to every purpose under heaven.
> (Ecclesiastes 3:1 KJV)

IMMEDIATELY AFTER DWIGHT'S death, the attending Doctor, my family, Sister Pasty, and Lesa took me to see Dwight. The Doctor gave me Dwight's wedding ring in a very small hospital hazardous bag. I had only seen the process of handing over another person's belongings on television, but this was reality. Dwight loved to wear his ring and never left home without it. Now, it was in a hazardous bag.

Dwight was proud of his ring and honored the promise we made to each other until death did us part. As I continue the grieving process, I continue to wear Dwight's wedding band around my neck on a chain that was given to me by Sarai. The season for Dwight wearing his ring has ended, but the memories linger in my heart every day.

I know God is continuing to bless us daily. God is working miracles to restore us to a place beyond what we can imagine into complete healing and restoration. Therefore, let us continue to magnify the Lord as we go through our process of healing.

Reflective Questions:

Am I allowing God to lead me into this new season as I cherish the memories of my previous season together?

How has God used these precious memories to help me move forward on my journey toward healing?

_____

_____

Pray:

Our Father, Who Art In Heaven, Hallowed Be Thy Name. Father, I thank You for each season of my life. Sometimes during a stormy season like this, I am weak and need Your strength. Lord, thank You for Our Shepherd, the One I am depending on to lead me as I walk this journey in my current season. Amen.

Day 2
Stepping Out In Faith–The Wedding

> There is no fear in love. But perfect love drives out fear, because fear has to do with punishment. The one who fears is not made perfect in love. (1 John 4:18 NIV)

FAMILY MEMBERS FROM across the globe—London, Canada, The Turks & Caicos Islands, and the United States of America came to the islands of The Bahamas to celebrate the marriage of Anthony (Mirage) my nephew and Robyn his bride to be.

It was such a special time for my family as we were truly taken aback by the sudden passing of Dwight. We needed something that was fun and not sad. This was my first event with family and friends, a wedding of all things. Even though I rose up as a woman of God, I got dressed nervously, gently applying make-up. I was going to a wedding for the first time in seventeen years without Dwight.

I guessed I would walk in supernatural authority, but I was moving slowly. Carol came and made sure I got dressed. We arrived at the wedding, and it was the best step I had taken in my grief journey. I enjoyed myself at the wedding. I had no immediate grief as I rejoiced with the family over this beautiful couple. It was a few days later that it hit me how God and I had attended the wedding together that day.

Reflective Question:

What is God challenging you to do with Him as you move forward to become the woman He has called you to be?

_____

_____

Pray:

Father, I thank You for being a covenant keeper whose promises are true and pure. Lord, I'm thanking You for helping me to deal with my brokenness as I work towards becoming the woman You created me to be. Thank You, Lord, for a bounce-back personality that is moving me forward on this journey. Amen

Day 3
The Sudden Rain
Brings Forth a Sudden Outburst

He also said to the crowds, "When you see a cloud rising in the west, you say at once, 'A shower is coming' and it happens." (Luke 12:54 ESV)

When I walked out of the house to begin a new work week, I felt a heaviness come over me. I knew it was going to be a downpour, but I continued on my journey stopping at mommy's house before 8 a.m. However, this morning, I did not sit and chat with her. I told mommy the clouds were dark and the heavy rain was coming soon. I wanted to get to work before the parking lot got flooded.

Within a few seconds, though, the thunder and lightning started bringing with it a heavy downpour. It was raining so hard, it was a slow, long drive to work. The parking lot was flooded. As I sat there, I heard the familiar voice in my spirit. Dwight was calling and questioning my whereabouts.

"I'm at the office," I always answered, letting him know I had arrived safely in spite of the heavy rain. Then, he would give me strict instructions not to leave the building until the rain let up.

I would respond, "Okay, honey, I am staying put."

As I sat in the vehicle, I was unable to move as my tears just came from nowhere. Suddenly, I could see clearly the rain was gone. My tears were tears of love and joy as I remembered how much Dwight had shown me how much he loved me. For a man to express love like this and leave a lasting memory is unexplainable.

This was God at work, not washing away the memories but refreshing my spirit. I was reminded how it is better to love and lose than not to have loved at all.

Are you willing to receive the refreshing in your spirit as God washes over you with special memories of that special love?

Don't suppress those beautiful memories, cherish them, and thank God for reminding you of His love as well. Record those refreshing memories and add to them often.

Pray:

Spirit of the Living God, thank You for the showers of blessings You provided this morning, not only to remind me about how much You love me, but also to remind me about how much Dwight and I loved each other. Thank You, for the refreshing You sent to me. Amen.

Day 4
Pray Without Ceasing

Pray without ceasing. In everything give thanks: for this is the will of God in Christ Jesus concerning you.
(1 Thessalonians 5:17-18 KJV)

I was feeling overwhelmed at work. I wished my cell phone would ring and I would get one of Dwight's well-timed calls saying, "I'm checking on you, Joyce. Is everything okay?" He always seemed to know when I desperately needed to hear his voice and words of encouragement. Today, though, the call would not come.

Suddenly, the cell phone beeped. I was a bit annoyed as I vigorously tried to complete the task at hand. I had no time to talk, but as I glanced towards the beep, I read "pray." In obedience to the "call," I bowed my head and prayed. Dwight did not call, but I received a divine call to enter into God's presence. As I opened my eyes, it was as if I was seeing God at work while I was at work. I do not recall when that overwhelmed feeling left me, but I was at peace and worked calmly to complete the task at hand. I do not recall when I set my cell phone alarm to remind me to pray, but I know God knew just what I needed.

When you have one of those days where the world seems to be closing in all around you, why not take a break, bow your head, close your eyes, and spend a few minutes in the presence of your heavenly Father?

He is waiting to take you in His arms and flood you with a sense of peace only He can give you.

Pray:

Thank You, Lord Jesus, for aligning my needs to Your will. Thank You for using even the cell phone to be spiritually aware of Your continuous presence, not only when I have issues but remind me to pray without ceasing. God help me to know that You are always a promise keeper and just a prayer away. Amen.

Day 5
Accept Kind Words–Words of Encouragement

> Finally, all of you, be like-minded, be sympathetic, love one another, be compassionate and humble. (1 Peter 3:8 NIV)

To be truthful people have been compassionate and often expressed their own sadness for my situation. Often, they were genuine and cried, some sat silently with me just letting me know they were supporting me, while others said the wrong things. I believe they just did not know what to say. Within myself, I knew it was just a natural response. They either did not know how to act or what to say. By the grace of God, I was able to communicate either non-verbally or verbally with those who offered me loving comfort in my grief. I know some people have experienced grief from a distance and can only communicate what they know.

The grief process is difficult, but we must keep going forward. Don't even think about turning around even when you walk into a room and see others whispering, knowing they are discussing your situation. You must keep going forward and receive those kind and encouraging words.

Most people have a true desire to comfort others suffering in grief, though most do not know how to achieve it. Those who have experienced it often know that just being there for a grieving friend is what they really need. Receive from them and thank God for those who are there for you.

Be that kind of friend when you see others who are in need of comfort and encouragement.

Pray:

Dear Lord, I thank You for allowing me to accept people who are genuine in expressing their feelings. Father God in heaven, I pray You would reach each individual where there is a need and bless them as they show brotherly love towards one another. Amen.

Day 6
My Journal
God's Perfect Love

> There is no fear in love. But perfect love drives out fear, because fear has to do with punishment. The one who fears is not made perfect in love. (1 John 4:18 NIV)

As I wrote this week's passages, I realized walking with God has helped me to move forward so I can help others by sharing His faithfulness.

As you journeyed with me this week through the stages of my grief, think about where your journey with God has taken you. Review the scriptures from this week and record how they have given you what you need to continue moving forward.

_____

_____

_____

_____

_____

STAGE 4 OF GRIEF
Depression

WE OFTEN THINK we are depressed when a grief event first occurs, but there is usually a lot of shock and other emotions present before any real depression can set in. The signs of depression due to grief usually appear when a sense of finality is realized. Depression due to grief is technically episodic, even though it may last for a lengthy period of time.[8]

The depressive stage feels as though it will last forever. We withdraw from life and feel overwhelmed, helpless, and lack energy.

> "Grief is not just a series of events, stages, or timelines. Our society places enormous pressure on us to get over loss, to get through grief. But how long do you grieve for a husband of fifty years, a teenager killed in a car accident, a four-year-old child: a year? Five years? Forever? The loss happens in time, in fact in a moment, but its aftermath lasts a lifetime."
>
> — Elisabeth Kubler-Ross

WEEK FOUR
DAY 1
Look Your Best At All Times

I praise you because I am fearfully and wonderfully made. (Psalm 139:14 NIV)

TODAY, I AM feeling the presence of the Holy Spirit. I am also expecting something will happen in my life as I begin my day. I am feeling and looking really good. My nails, hair, and clothing are on point. During my grief, I have gotten several wonderful comments about my appearance.

Now, for some strange reason, people will compliment me. Most are genuine, but sometimes when I have not seen someone since the passing of Dwight, they would say, "But you look so good."

There is a myth that once you are experiencing grief, you should look broke, busted, and disgusted. This is so far from the truth as the Bible cites that we are created in God's image, and we are His ambassadors on earth.

If I believe my outer appearance is reflecting what's in my heart including owning who I am and where I am not ashamed of my grief or being widowed. By accepting my fate and pushing forward by transforming my mind and dressing to ensure I do not look the way I am feeling.

Reflective Questions:

Am I dressing to ensure I do not look the way I am feeling?

Am I reflecting God's image as an ambassador for Him?

What changes do I need to make in my attire and my demeanor to truly own who I am?

_____

_____

Pray:

Our Father who art in heaven, thank You for perfecting everything that concerns me so that I am prepared and fully equipped to walk in Your authority and be able to renew my mind, and spirit, and to live out the plans that You have willed for me. Amen

Day 2
Walking in God's Natural Light

> The one who says he resides in God ought himself to walk as Jesus walked. (1 John 2:6 NASB)

As I continue to strive toward living life according to God's purpose and plan for my life, I have incorporated walking as a part of my mental, physical, and spiritual life. Taking care of my physical health gives me the edge I need to walk in God's presence. When I am walking, I am physically strengthened, I am refreshed, and it gives my mental health a boost. Of course, I sleep better, and it seems my waist is getting smaller, but I am not sure.

Despite the challenges of life, I took one difficult, struggling, and slow step walking in the fullness of God's grace and mercies.

Taking one step at a time and increasing steps as time goes on will help with the grieving process. I often remind myself, "Greater is He that is within me than he that is in the world" (1 John 4:4). That is what I call inner strength, and this causes me to be able to focus and finish on the path He has guided me to and not walk across the center.

Instead of withdrawing from life and allowing helplessness to drain my energy, I choose to go outside and walk with Him in His natural healing light.

Reflective Question:

Will you take this one step today and begin to let Him bathe you in His natural healing light?

As you walk, share your thoughts with your loving Heavenly Father and allow Him to fill you with His energizing presence.

Record what each walk brings you as you spend this time with Him.

_____

_____

_____

_____

Pray:

Father God in heaven, I thank You for strengthening me when I am weak. Thank You, Lord, for walking with me as my Father when I am alone. Thank You, God, for Your presence because You are my God and Savior. Amen.

DAY 3
Reflection on God-Answered Prayers

Hear, O Lord, When I cry with my voice: have mercy also upon me, and answer me. (Psalm 27:7 KJV)

WHY DID I put the number in my cellular telephone for the memorial gardens where the remains of Dwight lay? As I pondered on whether to answer the phone, I got extremely nervous and answered the dreaded call that Dwight's headstone had arrived.

To my surprise, the caller said she did not have good news, and since Father's Day was approaching she was offering me a vase to put on Dwight's temporary headstone. We agreed I would collect the vase on Monday. It was such an awful feeling as I visited Dwight that bright sunny morning. Tears were overflowing as I stood there still not understanding why. I cried and said, "God, I know You love me."

I walked slowly to my car and sat for a while. Finally, I drove a long distance in silence. As I approached my destination, I turned on the radio and the song, "So You Would Know" by the Brooklyn Tabernacle Choir was playing. I knew in my inner self God was sending me a clear message that

Day 3

He has proven Himself over and over again showing me how much He loves me. In a daze, I sat in my vehicle waiting for the song to finish. It is amazing that God answered my cry. God saw my heart was still broken.

Then He asked, "How many times must I prove My love to you?"

Reflective Questions:

Is God asking you this question today?

Reflect on and write out the ways He has shown His love for you in the past and thank Him for always being there for you.

_____

_____

_____

Pray:

Father, thank You for reflections and reminders when I forget how You are always close to the broken-hearted. Help me, Lord, to not only focus on the difficulties of life but to have hope in You knowing You continually show Your love for me. Amen.

DAY 4
Trusting God to Take Care of My Needs

But my God shall supply all your needs according to his riches in glory in Christ Jesus. (Philippians 4:19 KJV)

IT HAD BEEN such an awful feeling as I visited Dwight that day. Tears were overflowing. On my way home, I turned on the radio and the song, "So You Would Know" by the Brooklyn Tabernacle Choir was playing. God sent me a message that day on how He had proven Himself faithful over and over again and that I needed to continue to trust Him.

After I heard that song as I was driving home, I felt as if I had disappointed God. I have played that song daily since that day because it reminds me of how God truly takes care of me in every situation.

REFLECTIVE QUESTIONS:

Do my actions show my loving heavenly Father that I trust Him to take care of needs whether they are physical, mental, or spiritual?

Day 4

As you pray, remind yourself of His great love for you and His many ways of reassuring you, especially in the midst of your grief.

Pray:

Father, thank You for Your everlasting love and concern for me. Forgive me for not always trusting You even though I can see clearly every day how You take good care of me. I see how You have opened doors and granted me divine favor. Father, thank You for how You have granted me wisdom to discern and follow the direction of the Holy Spirit. Father, I present myself under Your authority. Please forgive my sinful ways and renew in me a right spirit. In Jesus' Name, Amen.

Day 5
Dad's First Father's Day
and Dwight's Death Anniversary

> I am the vine, ye are the branches: he that abideth in me, and I in him, the same bringeth forth much fruit: for without me ye can do nothing. (John 15:5 KJV)

I DESCRIBE THE year ending June 2022 as a season of peaks and valleys. Dwight's death anniversary would come whether I welcomed it or not. My father had died two years earlier and Father's Day was also fast approaching. I now had to deal with my unresolved grief with my father, William H. Seymour, and my husband, Dwight whom I often called dad as Sarai, my family and her friends did.

They both enjoyed the attention given on Father's Day, but preferred to stay out of the limelight. Sarai presented dad with his father's day gifts. He hugged her so tightly that they both laughed. She told him she shopped for him making sure the bag would be filled and running over. I know Sarai and I never thought that would be the last Father's Day hug she would receive from dad.

Day 5

As what appeared to be a dreadful time approached, I felt uneasy and grieved. I would relive both days when death occurred with the two men I loved so dearly.

Reflective Questions:

What does God want you to do so you can face this day? Can you trust the process?

Family and friends suggested I go live with mom for the week, go to the spa, or have lunch with friends, but they advised me not to spend time alone. Instead, I parked my vehicle and stayed at home. However, I never felt alone. I knew I had to have complete dependence on God while at the same time continue to build my faith in the valley.

I pulled myself together and got dressed smartly a few days before Father's Day. I visited Dwight's gravesite alone. I just could not bear the thought of visiting my father at the same time. It was just difficult. I felt awful as streams of tears like a waterfall burst down my face. However, I truly felt God's presence. I knew it would be the only way I could survive this journey. I had to stand on God's divine promise He would never leave me. I had to trust the process and continue to hold on to God's unchanging hands with a courageous spirit so I could survive and walk into this new season God has proposed for me. I trust I will soon understand why I was chosen for a journey of taking one day at a time while walking one step at a time. I learned it's not wise to rush the grief process as this will only delay the healing. I empower myself daily with praise, worship, and staying in the presence of God.

As I communicated and cried with Dwight, I knew he could not hear me, but God could. I motioned to the worker and humbly requested he clean Dwight's gravesite, especially around the temporary stone. A year later, I had not received Dwight's headstone.

On Father's Day, I visited dad's gravesite with Pamela. How she loved dad. We placed a bouquet of bright yellow flowers on dad's headstone. Two days later, it was the first anniversary of Dwight's death. Kendia, Sarai on video, and I visited Dwight's gravesite. It was unreal.

Pray:

Spirit of the living God, please fall afresh on me. Renew a right spirit and restore within me a desire to press forward in the things of Jesus Christ. I will not faint but hold onto Your promises with hope as You perfect that which concerns me. Grant me, dear Lord, strength, and energy to handle life's challenges as I move along my life's journey. Amen.

Day 6
My Journal

GRIEF IS A powerful emotion that can shake even the strongest person. The confusion, chaos, and inner turmoil that result can sweep you away from productivity and plans for the future. It can drive you to a place of despair and depression. Family and friends may find it hard to relate to the feelings you experience in this place of grief. However, God has promised He will never leave you to walk this journey alone

Review what I shared this week on my journey and apply what helps you with your journey.

_____

_____

_____

_____

_____

_____

_____

STAGE 5 OF GRIEF
Acceptance

THE PERSON EXPERIENCING grief no longer is looking backward to try and recover the life they once had with the deceased. It is not to say they no longer feel the vast array of emotions brought on by their grief, but they are ready to embrace the idea they are reaching a new point in their lives and beginning to understand there is a new beginning on the horizon.

At first, we may want to maintain life as it was before our loved one died. However, we see that we cannot maintain the past intact. It has been forever changed and we must readjust. Finding acceptance may be just having more good days than bad ones. As we begin to live again and enjoy our life, we often feel we are betraying our loved ones. Instead of denying our feelings, we listen to our needs; we move, change, grow, and evolve. We may start to reach out to others and become involved in their lives. We begin to live again, but we cannot do so until we have given grief its time.

Week Five:
Day 1
Meditate, Trust, and be Still

> Keep this Book of the Law always on your lips; meditate on it day and night, so that you may be careful to do everything written in it. Then you will be prosperous and successful. (Joshua 1:8 NIV)

THIS GRIEF JOURNEY has been one where I am empowered by the Holy Spirit as I meditate on God's word daily and at odd times when I need reassurance. I know God is always near, and I need not be ashamed of talking to Him anyplace and at any time. Even in the wee hours of the morning when I cannot sleep, I reach for the Bible and my sleep becomes peaceful. Whatever disturbs my sleep, I cast it on the Lord.

When I am faced with any decision I reference biblical verses this refresh my mind, body, and spirit. It ignites a spirit of wisdom, knowledge, and understanding, and gives me clarification on matters that I do not understand. The Holy Spirit gives me direction on how to make the best choices. Sometimes it is in the midst of counsel.

The Holy Spirit just comes when you least expect Him, and God's destiny helpers are waiting for you to show up. I am not saying there will not be challenges, but it will still work itself out when we cast our concerns on the Lord. Most times it calls for us just to follow the still small voice, be obedient, and stand still.

The Holy Spirit opens doors of opportunity, and divine and supernatural favor takes place when you walk with His Word in your heart. God grants a surprise in every situation, though not always what we expect. We are reassured and prove it is the best decision for us at that time.

Trust the process. God is working it out. God is faithful and He promises in His Word never to withhold any good thing from us if we continue to walk uprightly. Always striving to please Him.

Reflective Questions:

Are you trusting the process?
Are you striving to please God?
Are you meditating on His Word daily so you know what His will for your life is as you move forward on your journey with Him?

Pray:

Father, I thank You today for Your unfailing love and care. Thank You for showing me how to trust You and the process

Week Five:

no matter how difficult it would be. Father, help me to accept that the answer might be "no" sometimes and to be reminded that the best is just ahead. Give me the strength when I fall to continue to meditate on Your Word daily. Amen.

Day 2
Managing Your Finances Begins With God

> Honor the Lord with your wealth and with the firstfruits of all your produce, then your barns will be filled with plenty, and your vats will be bursting with wine. (Proverbs 3:9-10 ESV)

My twenty-year career in finances involved budgeting, executing, and monitoring billions of dollars where I was held accountable. However, when it comes to my own money, I am accountable only to myself for the most part. Though I do not have a financial plan or an emergency fund stashed aside, this was not Dwight's style. He always believed in being prepared for a rainy financial day.

We understood we were to honor the Lord with our wealth before all of our expenses were paid. Our priority was to tithe first then pay the bills and honor God with our first fruit. It is an expression of our love for God and confirms our commitment to contributing to the building of God's kingdom.

Day 2

This is when the chain reaction takes place. Deuteronomy 7:9 and Psalm 105:8 both confirm God is faithful to those who keep His covenant for a thousand generations.

One day, as I was delivering teenage novels to my nieces, the Holy Spirit said to check those books, but I didn't know what I was looking for as I began to check the novels. Apparently, I did not thoroughly check because when I delivered the novels and my nieces began selecting their books, I noticed a piece of paper peeking out. As I opened the book, I read the word tithe in Dwight's handwriting. To my surprise, it was five hundred and seventy-five dollars and clearly marked tithe. Even after his death, Dwight left his final tithe. I did not even think twice about keeping these funds or battling in my spirit over what to do as I knew it belonged to God. God's promises are real and will open the windows of heaven.

Reflective Questions:

Do you faithfully obey God's directions concerning tithes, offerings, and gifts to further His kingdom's work?

Pray:

Father God, help me to study and understand Your Word so I will be obedient to Your directions and my soul may be satisfied with Your many blessings as I sing Your praises and talk about Your marvelous works. In Jesus' name, I pray. Amen

DAY 3
Complete the Assignment God Birthed in You

> Prepare thy work without, and make it fit for thyself in the field; and afterwards build thine house. (Proverbs 24:27 KJV)

THIS SCRIPTURE IS prophetic as I recall after Dwight's death I just did not know what to do with myself. How do I move forward? One thing I can say is that I loved being at home alone where I was always at peace. This is where I felt God's presence so strongly.

Yet, as I grieved with sleeplessness thinking of my unresolved grief of my dad, now compounded with Dwight's death.

Dwight was my grief therapist. He encouraged me as we grew in God's grace. We saw the manifestation of healing and deliverance taking place. I am now depending more on the guidance of the Holy Spirit.

Under the anointing of the Holy Spirit, I decided to write and publish my grief journal to share with others. With the help of the Lord, writing this journal has helped me to heal and accept my brokenness. It has helped me work through my grief by taking full responsibility for my future and taking the first step to begin a global grief ministry.

Day 3

The scripture that has encouraged me as I journal and depend on God for wisdom and motivation has been Proverbs 11:25. "The liberal soul shall be made fat and he that watereth shall be watered himself" (KJV).

I stretch my faith in the hope it will affirm others to take one step towards God's purpose for their lives each day. It will also remind us that when we weep, Jesus is moved in the spirit. He has heard our cries and declared that everything is going to be alright.

We will smile again and deliverance will come by the power of the Holy Spirit.

Reflective Questions:

Will you take that first step toward fulfilling the assignment God now has for you even as you walk through this grief journey with Him?

Pray:

Father, I thank You for guiding me through the process of healing as I journal my daily thoughts to help others. Father, I thank You that someone will be touched, their inner spirit will be revived, and their strength will be fully restored. In the precious name of Jesus Christ, Amen.

Day 4
God's Promises of Grace Unto Old Age

Now also when I am old and gray headed, O God, forsake me not; until I have shew thy strength unto this generation, and thy power to everyone that is to come. (Psalm 71:18 KJV)

I ALWAYS IMAGINED Dwight and I would grow old together, walking, watching movies that Dwight selected for both of us to enjoy as our choices were so different, laughing and dancing while Sarai rolled her eyes as she thought her parents should not be lovey-dovey. So many fond memories such as Dwight's radiant smile, his caring spirit, and our regular lunch dates. He was a great father and husband, and a fun traveling partner. He would eat what I cooked and say, "This is very tasty." Smiling, he would add, "Joyce it's so good." When I baked bread, he'd say, "I could smell how good it tasted." In no time it was all gone.

Dwight loved organizing the linen closet. A year later, I have not touched Dwight's linen closet. I can recall how he looked forward to refolding the towels the way his mama taught him. Honestly, I just let him have his way.

Day 4

Growing old together was not God's plan for us. Yet, I believe that even alone I shall bring forth fruit and will flourish as long as God's grace and mercy are granted to me. I know God has a plan for my life as I strive to become the best version of myself and become who God has purposed and planned for me.

As your pray today, ask God to show you what He has purposed for you as you strive to become all that He has planned for you. List how He answers your prayer.

_____

_____

_____

Pray:

Dear God, I thank You for my life, health, and strength. Thank You, Lord, for the beautiful memories my loved one and I created and that I can hold dear to my heart. God, I thank You for the promise You will not forsake me. Help me to show Your strength to this generation. O God, I asked You not to cast me off in old age and as I grieve over my loss. In Jesus' name, I pray. Amen.

Day 5
The First Step

And the God of all grace, who called you to His eternal glory in Christ, after you have suffered a little while, will Himself restore you and make you strong, firm and steadfast. (1 Peter 5:10 NIV)

Zechariah 4:10 states we must not despise small beginnings. In keeping with God's instructions, I decided I had to take tiny steps to begin my recovery. My steps reminded me of a proverb I once heard that asked, "How do you eat an elephant?" The answer was, "Just take one bite at a time." As I envisioned myself alongside this analogy, my destination still seemed impossible to reach.

However, I knew I had to keep walking so I would reach my divine purpose. At this time, I did not know what my divine purpose was, but I knew God had a plan. As I continued towards the destination where God knew I was to reach, I began to trust Him more and more. My faith and hope grew with each tiny step I took in obedience to His direction.

Day 5

Additional steps have been added to this new path of my life as I have walked the sandy beach near the shoreline, climbed the steps of victory, and ran down some slippery slopes and up some rocky hills. Now I know it is okay to take baby steps. Each is such a great and awesome accomplishment.

Amazingly, without even realizing it, my steps have become giant faith leaps filled with hope, dreams, and appreciating the true meaning of life's small steps.

Reflective Questions:

Are you ready to begin the next part of your journey?

Will you step out in faith and take those first small steps?

As your steps become leaps of faith, record the hopes and dreams God is revealing to you.

_____

_____

_____

Pray:

Father God, thank You for restoring my energy to begin my first step. Lord, encourage me to have a willing spirit. Thank

You for restoring my health so my journey will continue and one day I will jog into new victory. Thank You, Lord. Amen.

Day 6
My Journal

As you complete this month-long journey with me, think back over what God has revealed to you in your journey.

Record what has impacted you the most and how you are going to use what you have learned to move forward as God leads you on the next phase of your journey.

_____

_____

_____

_____

_____

_____

_____

_____

_____

_____

Final Word
It's Not the End
It's a New Beginning

> But the God of all grace, who hath called us into His eternal glory by Christ Jesus, after that ye have suffered a while, make you perfect, stablish, strengthen, settle you. (1 Peter 5:10)

WHEN I FIRST started journaling my thoughts, they were designed to help others navigate through the grief healing process with God at the center and with the help of God's amazing grace. I was extremely vulnerable myself at the time, but miraculously, this journal provided so much relief for me personally. I am glad I was obedient to the voice of God and stepped out in faith believing this journal will reach worldwide.

Proverbs 3:6 says, "In all thy ways acknowledge Him and He shall direct thy path" (KJV). Truly God has directed my thoughts and steps during this season. I felt the presence of God with each word typed. Even if I had 10,000 words; it would not be enough to describe how grateful I am to God for allowing me this opportunity to serve others who are grieving.

Final Word

The end of this journal is really a new beginning. To be successful to the end of our life's journey, we must persevere. As an athlete runs the race to win the prize, we realize the race is not always won the first time. We must race, walk, and dive toward the finish line with God at our side.

As long as we trust God wholeheartedly, the burden gets lighter as we shift to deal with each circumstance. I know the Lord will grant us grace to endure. The Lord will not withhold any good thing from us as we walk uprightly (see Psalm 84:11).

Let's keep moving forward.

Pray:

Heavenly Father, I humbly ask that when we encounter life's circumstances, we are always reminded we are not alone. Lord, help us to realize the challenges of life are designed to remind us that sometimes, You are repositioning us for newness and we must trust the process of renewal.
Increase our faith to trust the outcome and hold onto Your promise that after we have suffered a while, You will perfect that which concerns us and strengthen us to undertake the new journey You have set before us. Amen.

About the Author

JOYCELYN V. GILBERT has a Bachelor of Science Degree in Business Administration, Bethune Cookman College, and Masters of Business Administration with concentration in Financial Management, City University of Seattle, Washington, USA, and to enhance her knowledge and understanding of youth issues, she became a Certified Youth Officer and obtained a certificate in Trauma Informed Care (Youth).

Mrs. Gilbert is employed as a Senior Director of Finance and previously served as a member of her local church Women's Discipleship Ministry and on the church's finance fundraising committee.

During her spare time, she enjoys daily walks while basking in the presence of the Lord, reading, baking, and cooking.

ENDNOTES

[1] "The Five Stages of Grief," FuneralResources.com, 2015, https://funeralresources.com/grief-and-loss/five-stages-of-grief/.

[2] Ibid.

[3] Matthew 6:25-34, *New American Standard Bible (NASB)* Copyright© 1960, 1962, 1963, 1968, 1971, 1972, 1973, 1975, 1977, 1995 by The Lockman Foundation.

[4] "The Five Stages of Grief," FuneralResources.com, 2015, https://funeralresources.com/grief-and-loss/five-stages-of-grief/.

[5] Kate McGahan (Jack McAfghan), *Return from Rainbow Bridge: An Afterlife Story of Loss, Love and Renewal,* Goodreads, https://www.goodreads.com/quotes/8183590-the-fact-is-that-when-you-admit-that-you-can-t.

[6] "The Five Stages of Grief," FuneralResources.com, 2015, https://funeralresources.com/grief-and-loss/five-stages-of-grief/.

[7] Dana Arcuri, *Sacred Wandering: Growing Your Faith In The Dark,* May 25, 2019, https://www.goodreads.com/book/show/46020234-sacred-wandering?ac=1&from_search=true&qid=W-88b564yyZ&rank=4.

[8] "The Five Stages of Grief," FuneralResources.com, 2015, https://funeralresources.com/grief-and-loss/five-stages-of-grief/.

www.ingramcontent.com/pod-product-compliance
Ingram Content Group UK Ltd.
Pitfield, Milton Keynes, MK11 3LW, UK
UKHW041944230426
12048UKWH00008B/120